IMAGES
of America

GLOUCESTER
ON THE WIND
AMERICA'S GREATEST FISHING PORT
IN THE DAYS OF SAIL

THEY THAT GO DOWN TO THE SEA IN SHIPS

IMAGES
of America

GLOUCESTER
ON THE WIND
AMERICA'S GREATEST FISHING PORT
IN THE DAYS OF SAIL

Joseph E. Garland

ARCADIA

First published 1995
Copyright © Joseph E. Garland 1995

ISBN 0 7524 0079 7

Published by Arcadia Publishing,
an imprint of the Chalford Publishing Corporation
One Washington Center, Dover, New Hampshire 03820
Printed in Great Britain

All photographs are from the Gordon W. Thomas Collection of the Cape Ann Historical
Association, with its generous permission, unless otherwise noted.

Cover photograph by Chester L. Morrissey (author's collection)

In Memoriam
Sterling Hayden
Actor, writer, schoonerman and wanderer,
for whom Gloucester was as close to home
as he ever got

Contents

Introduction		7
1.	"She Scoons!"	9
2.	Fitting Out	13
3.	Outward Bound	29
4.	Dorymates	49
5.	The Georgesmen	63
6.	Seines, Sloops, and Swordfish	69
7.	Back Home	79
8.	Taking In the Slack	93
9.	Winter	107
10.	Shipshape and Gloucester Fashion	113
11.	Masters and Men	119
12.	The Romance of It	131
13.	Requiem	149
14.	Resurrection	153
Epilogue or Epitaph?		159
Sources		160

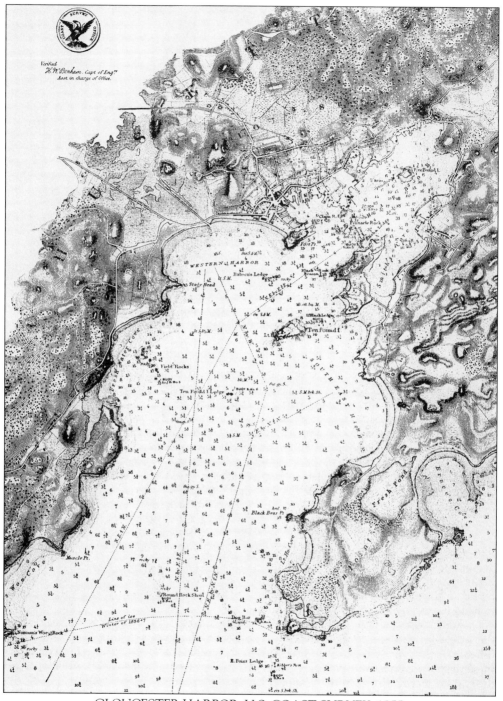

GLOUCESTER HARBOR, U.S. COAST SURVEY, 1855

Introduction

The fog had gone, but a sullen sea ran in great rollers behind it. The *We're Here* slid, as it were, into long, sunk avenues and ditches which felt quite sheltered and homelike if they would only stay still; but they changed without rest or mercy, and flung up the schooner to crown one peak of a thousand gray hills, while the wind hooted through her rigging as she zigzagged down the slopes.

Captains Courageous
Rudyard Kipling

No chapter in America's hectic history has been shut with such a snap as Gloucester's. After three hundred years of fishing the richest banks of the Atlantic, under no power but the wind's—with no help but a sextant, compass, taffrail log, sounding lead, and sea sense—the end came suddenly; in the forty years since the last schooner unloaded the last trip of hand-caught codfish, overkill, greed, and neglect have endangered to the brink of extinction what until too recently was taken for granted as the inexhaustible bounty of the sea.

Nowhere in the Western Hemisphere was that reckless romance with wind and wave pursued more fruitfully or more fatefully than from this Beau Port. Discovered on the edge of the wilderness and named by Samuel de Champlain in 1606, it was settled in 1623 by fishermen from Dorchester and then Gloucester (in the west of old England). Here on the shore of New England was planted the first outpost of the Crown's Colony of Massachusetts Bay.

A century ago upwards of four hundred of Gloucester's uniquely beautiful two-masted schooners sailed forth to the northwest Atlantic fishing grounds from Virginia to Greenland. Thrashing year-round through seas infamous for their treachery, tens of thousands of brave and hardy fishermen returned to market with hundreds of millions of fish, every resisting ounce pulled up from the bottom with hook and line, or brought over the rail, inch by straining inch, in hand-hauled nets.

No kind fate decrees that those who go to sea return: during the romanticized "glory days" of the windships between 1830 and 1900—a mere fifth of Gloucester's history—3,800 of her fishermen never sailed back around Eastern Point, nor did 670 of her schooners. The toll of these years alone on a town averaging but 17,000 souls exceeded by more than seventy percent the entire American losses in the War of 1812.

What kind of a price is this to pay for the bounty of the Lord, for feeding hungry mouths? What sort of compact did these men make, they who went down to the sea? The object of this work is to invoke a vision, albeit fragmentary, of a departed and poignantly recent past as a reminder to those of us who are the inheritors and beneficiaries of what only a rapidly dwindling band remembers at all. The reality of that vision is defined, limited, and by its nature distorted by the photographic montage that I (whose family blood is in the shallow soil here, yet who like everyone else remembers so very little, and who has never gone fishing) have selected.

Perhaps my view as a Gloucester writer is no less idiosyncratic, after all, than whatever motivated the dozens of photographers whose work appears here to aim their old-fashioned cameras at this or that at a particular moment on a particular day in whatever year. Nor does it really matter.

What does matter is that this sorrowful, hopeful birthplace of the American fisheries has survived lean times and times of plenty, writers, photographers, and artists by the thousands, summer folks by the tens of thousands, tourists by the millions, and even its fishermen. Surprisingly, much of our sprawling, sea-girt, wilderness-embraced, saltmarsh-insinuated, glacier-forsaken, tide-licked place remains recognizably, if ever more tenuously, as it once was when clouds of sail scudded over the harbor. Beyond this, the legacy of the long voyages under the wind, which ruled every going and every coming and breathed life and death into every corner of the port from 1623 on, has become the province of the antiquarian and the archeologist.

Artists have a prominent place in preserving visions of Gloucester's past. In his twenty-five most productive years before he died in 1865, our mysterious Fitz Hugh Lane immortalized in his glowing oils the eerie luminescence of Gloucester Harbor and the still powerful presence of the fishermen and their schooners. Later the robust visitor Winslow Homer captured the romantic vitality and contrasting moods of subject and setting. Many lesser "knights and ladies of the brush" followed to make a pioneer summer art colony of the more or less oblivious old fishtown. None caught the feel of the schooners at sea, and of the fishermen (ghosts in his mind's eye), like my friend the late Tom Hoyne.

Photography, on the other hand, emerged from the Civil War as a documentary art. By the early 1870s stereoscopic views of the real Gloucester were being produced by Rogers and the Procter Brothers, newspaper publishers who were far ahead of their time in reporting on the doings and misdoings in this busiest of fishing ports. In the mid-1880s the definitive work on the fisheries was compiled by the U.S. Fish and Fisheries Commission with an exhaustively researched text and an entire volume of arresting illustrations. The apogee of sail in the 1890s inspired the indomitable Martha Rogers Harvey, the ever-watchful Ernest Blatchford, Chester Walen, and Henry Spooner (among others), who lugged cameras with up to 8x10-inch glass plate negatives around the waterfront, and a few years later Eben Parsons (with his pocket Kodak). Others such as Adolph Kupsinel recorded the bittersweet curtain call of the International Fishermen's Races of the 1920s and '30s. All created images of wondrous detail, depth, and artistry, valuable as objects of art and history and preserved in the archives of the Cape Ann Historical Association.

Rare was the hard-worked fisherman who brought a camera aboard, like Chet Morrissey (who sixty years later loaned me his negatives). Rarer still the prescience of a John Clayton, whose unparalleled chronicle of five trips in the last dory-fishing American schooner *Adventure* (in the postwar years, before she retired in 1953) remains the ultimate record of the end of the era.

"Share and share alike" was the sacred compact of the dorymen. Not just the bounty of the sea, and their labor and suffering and sacrifice and loss. And not merely with each other, but with the sea itself. "For the Lord gave, and the Lord hath taken away."

And indeed He hath.

Joseph E. Garland

One
"She Scoons!"

"THEN A SCOONER LET HER BE!", Captain Andrew Robinson responded to an excited onlooker when he launched the prototype at East Gloucester in 1713. Pictured is a primitive two-masted "Chebacco boat" of about 1790 built on the neighboring Chebacco, now Essex, River. (Goode, *The Fisheries and Fishery Industries of the United States*)

AT ANCHOR ON THE GRAND BANK, the crew of a "heeltapper" handlines for codfish early in the 1800s. Like an overturned shoe, these slow, sturdy old schooners were Marblehead's mainstay into the 1840s, when disastrous storms knocked the town out of the fisheries, and Gloucester moved into the lead. (Goode)

STEADIED UNDER REEFED MAINSAIL, a more advanced "sharpshooter" anchors on the shoals of Georges Bank in the 1840s to handline for the then plentiful halibut. With its sharper bow and sleeker lines, the fast new type rapidly evolved by the 1850s into the clipper schooner that dominated for the rest of the century. (Goode)

10

A GOOD, WEATHERLY SEA BOAT, the old-fashioned, double-ended "pinky" schooner, with pointed "pink" stern and deep outboard rudder, outlasted later types, and continued fishing New England waters and doing odd jobs for a hundred years into the early twentieth century. Half-hidden by her jib is the Pavilion Hotel, predecessor of the Tavern on what is now Stacy Boulevard.

A BROAD-BOSOMED PINKY rests at anchor in Gloucester around the 1880s, while the "gang has a gam up forrard in the eyes of her."

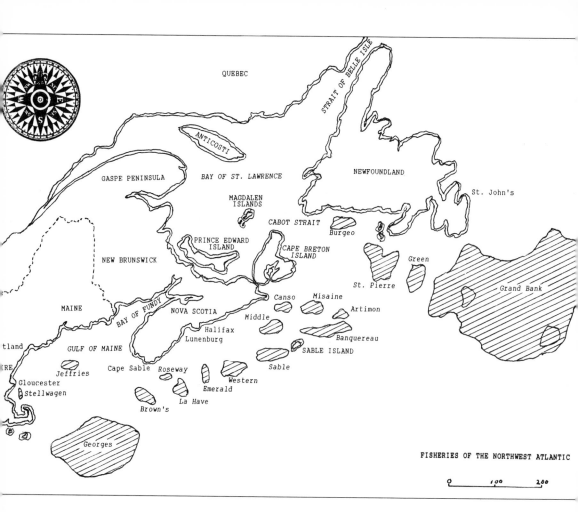

FISHERIES OF THE NORTHWEST ATLANTIC

Two

Fitting Out

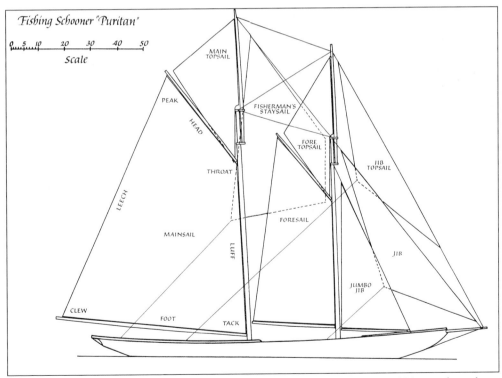

Fishing Schooner "Puritan"

0 5 10 20 30 40 50
Scale

MAIN
TOPSAIL

PEAK

HEAD

FISHERMAN'S
STAYSAIL

FORE
TOPSAIL

JIB
TOPSAIL

THROAT

LEECH

FORESAIL

MAINSAIL

LUFF

JIB

JUMBO
JIB

CLEW

FOOT

TACK

THE *PURITAN*, a creation of the great designer W. Starling Burgess in 1922, may have been the finest and fastest "Gloucesterman" ever built, but she didn't live long enough to prove it. (JEG, *Down to the Sea: The Fishing Schooners of Gloucester*)

SCHOONER DESIGN HAD COME A LONG WAY when the handsome *Nannie C. Bohlin* was built in John Bishop's yard at Vincent Cove. The keel for the next is being shaped and will be pried over to the ways after her launching on October 28, 1890. The pair of "shears" behind her bowsprit raised 90-foot masts vertically for stepping down through the deck.

BOWSPRIT SWUNG ABOARD (note the iron band at the end for the flying jibboom), the clipper schooner *Grace L. Fears* nears completion in David Alfred Story's yard on the west shore of the narrow entrance to Vincent Cove. Launched in July 1874, she went down with seven men in a December gale in 1897.

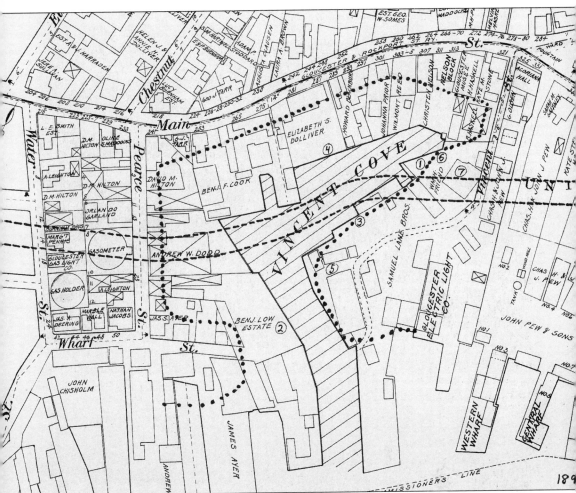

BURIED TODAY, Vincent Cove was bursting a hundred years ago, as can be seen in this 1899 Gloucester atlas. Innumerable wooden schooners, sloops, and small craft were built in the cramped yards of Daniel Poland, Charles Woodbury (1), "Dave Alf" Story (2), John Bishop (3), Thomas Irving (4) and others. Many of the vessels were of 110 feet and more waterline, and were launched into water bent around Vincent Point (5), which was hardly greater than 75 to 100 feet wide. Far larger in 1830, the Cove lapped at Main (then Spring) Street, following roughly the dotted line. Note the round-the-Cape electric trolley car tracks on Main Street. Today ghostly Vincent Cove—with its shipyards, Joe Call's spar yard (6), the original Cape Ann Anchor Works (7), lumber yards, coal pockets, fish plants, and all its hum and pounding of activity—lies under pavement and buildings, the victim of a hundred years of encroachment completed around World War I and sealed with the extension of Rogers Street (dashed lines) after the post-World War II final destruction of the old waterfront by Urban Renewal. The east side of Harbor Loop approximates Water Street. It is an archeologist's dream perhaps, but a preservationist's nightmare.

A COUPLE OF OLD-TIMERS spike home deck planking forward of the fish hatch at John Bishop's yard about 1910. Bulwark stanchions coming together at the bow await outside planking and rails and reveal the heft of the schooner's oak frames to which they're "sistered" (or fastened in vertical overlap).

MASTER SHIPBUILDER Thomas Irving (1832–1917) was also noted as a designer and maker of builder's models, examples of which are displayed at the Cape Ann Historical Museum.

WITH A MIGHTY WHOOSH the small schooner *Actor* slides down Tom Irving's cramped ways into Vincent Cove in 1902, so close to Main Street that the tower of city hall peeks over the rooftop above the men hanging on for dear life in the bow.

OVER IN ROCKPORT, which before 1840 was part of Gloucester called Sandy Bay, small shipbuilding flourished for many years after 1900 in the yard of David Waddell, whose ways ran dizzily out from the Bearskin Neck seawall over the town's miniature breakwatered harbor (shown at right). Waddell built numerous small schooners and other watercraft for Rockport's shore fishermen, who were based in the fishing shacks along the Neck and Pigeon Cove to the north, brave perches on a rocky and sea-smashed coast. (Joe Chetwynd collection)

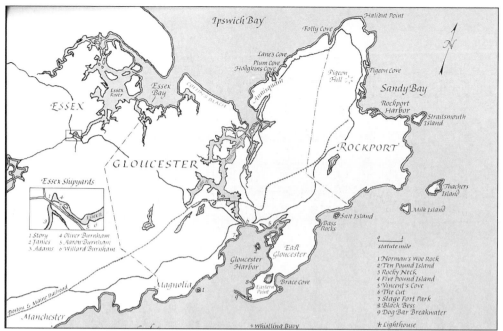

OVER 4,000 SHIPS, more per capita than anywhere else in the world, have been built in the rural backwater of Essex since the 1650s. New schooners were towed out the narrow, twisting river ahead of the outgoing tide, across Ipswich Bay and around Cape Ann to Gloucester Harbor for fitting-out. (JEG, *Down to the Sea*)

THE *PURITAN* SLIDES IN from the John F. James yard on March 15, 1922. Off fishing, she was so fast that Captain Jeff Thomas underestimated distance traveled and wrecked her on Nova Scotia's Sable Island bar in dense fog on June 23, 1922, with the loss of one of the crew. (Walter McNaney collection)

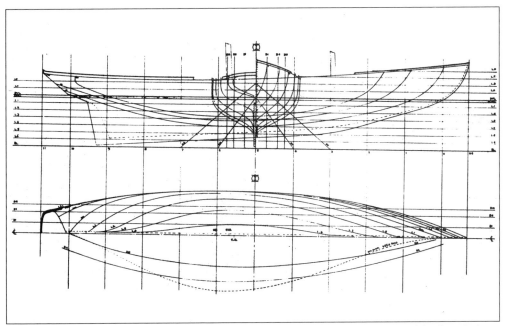

HER LINES REVEAL THE BEAUTY, STRENGTH, AND CHARACTER of the knockabout schooner *Adventure*, most famous of all the dory trawlers, designed by Thomas McManus and built for Jeff Thomas at the James yard in 1926. Today, she is a National Historic Landmark back in Gloucester. (JEG, *Adventure: Queen of the Windjammers*)

THE 60-FOOTER *NOKOMIS*, just launched from the James yard on March 12, 1903, heads out the Essex River for the long tow around to Gloucester. Lined off by the fisherman/designer George (Mel) McClain, she was lost with all hands a few years later in a hurricane. At least three more schooners can be seen on the ways.

NO MODEL T, all 139 feet of the *Henry Ford* from stem to stern zooms into the river from the yard of the famed Arthur D. Story on April 11, 1922. The *Henry Ford* was another McManus masterpiece. (Robert W. Phelps)

MEETING OF THE MASTERS (opposite page). At their peak in September 1916, Thomas F. McManus and Arthur D. Story, high priests of the golden age of the American fishing schooner, talk over their latest collaboration at A.D.'s yard in Essex Center. In the course of 430 vessel plans, McManus (who was largely self-taught) enhanced the safety, speed, comfort, and appearance of the schooner at its zenith, eliminating in his pioneering knockabout the "widowmaker" bowsprit from which untold men were swept by heavy seas while tending headsails. Story, the legendary and long-lived Essex builder, alone launched 397 wooden vessels of all types (predominantly fishing schooners) between 1880 and 1932, including some of the most famous in the history of the Gloucester fleet. His son Dana, and now his grandson Brad, carry on the Story tradition. (Walter McNaney collection)

BUT THE TOWLINE SNAPPED, and the *Henry Ford* drifted aground on Coffin's Beach (see map). It took 5 days for 3 tugs to float Captain Clayton Morrissey's big schooner, which drew close to 12 feet at the sternpost. (L. Francis Herreshoff)

ONCE LAUNCHED, the new schooner was fitted out for fishing in Gloucester, first by the sparmaker. Her "sticks" were hand-shaped from straight and tall pine, fir, or spruce. The *Henry Ford*'s mainmast was 90 feet by about 20 inches diameter at the base, foremast 84, maintopmast 52, and main boom 76 by a foot in diameter. George E. Thurston's spar yard, above and below, was at the head of Harbor Cove, south of the Town Landing on what is now St. Peter's Park. Tied up to Nauss's lumber wharf (above right) are small, engine-powered "Guinea boats" of the Sicilian fishermen who settled at Fort Point about 1900. (CAHA and *Master Mariners 1917 Yearbook*)

EVERY STITCH BY HAND, it took 45 (count 'em) sailmakers to keep up with the demand at Edward L. Rowe's loft alone, one of seven in Gloucester where after a three-week strike in 1899 the men won a nine-hour, three-dollar day. A big schooner could carry up to 10,000 square feet of cotton duck so thick it took a strong man to push a needle through. Rowe's was across Harbor Loop from the Star Fisheries parking lot. The 1847 Rockport Steam Cotton Mill at Dock Square employed 175 people and produced 3,000 yards of duck a day, besides twine and "India Rubber Cloth." The massive scantlings, or structural dimensions, of the schooners are revealed in the 1934 photograph (right) of two old hands "bending on" the throat of the mainsail to the main gaff. Note the size of mainmast, boom, and gaff above, and throat halyard blocks just overhead.

BLOCKS AND OARS of every size were the specialty of Harvey and Tarr at 89 Duncan Street along with about everything else in the way of ship's hardware. The leading chandlery for fishing gear was L.D. Lothrop (below) across and up the street; the founder invented the hand-cranked foghorn without which no Gloucesterman would sail. Arthur James English fish hooks were among the rarities to make inroads in Gloucester's integrated fishing industry, which included net and twine, fish box and oil clothing factories, and (in the old times) a ropewalk east of the Man at the Wheel statue and another behind the Sawyer Free Library between Middle and Prospect Streets.

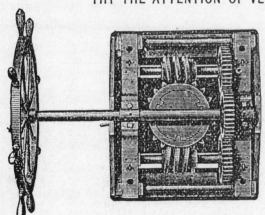
NATHAN RICHARDSON and his machine shop on Washington Street just south of the railroad crossing eventually conceded the field to A.P. Stoddart at 236 Main Street. No schooner was a genuine Gloucesterman without its big iron Stoddart wheel and gear. (Procter Brothers, *The Fisheries of Gloucester*)

25

SINCE 1793, THOUSANDS OF DORIES (most of them for the Gloucester fishing fleet) have emerged from Hiram Lowell's Boat Shop on the Merrimac River in Amesbury, now a National Historic Landmark. Fourteen to fifteen feet long (measured commonly on the bottom), the two-man "banks dory" had removable thwarts for "nesting" on the schooner's deck. "A pair of overalls were hung from a second-floor window to signal the Moultons [owners of the team] that a load of dories was ready," according to current owner James Odell. "If they were hung out the east end the load was for Gloucester, if the west, for Portsmouth." (Lowell's Boat Shop)

THE HEAVIEST GROUND TACKLE, required to hold 150 tons of bucking schooner in a gale, was home-made in the foundry of the Cape Ann Anchor Works, first located at Vincent Cove and later by the railroad bridge at the end of Whittemore Street. Big anchors, small anchors, and horseshoes galore were produced by the twenty-two blacksmiths in Gloucester in 1900. (Blatchford)

TRANSPLANTED CAPE CODDERS Isaac Higgins and Asa Gifford built 3,500 small craft between 1877 and 1892 alone, ranging from skiffs, dories, and sailboats to the classic double-ended mackerel seineboats they adapted from whaleboats (an example can be seen in the foreground behind the old-fashioned lobster pots). Their shop was on Parker Street south of today's Gloucester Supply.

HUNDREDS OF THOUSANDS of home-coopered barrels rolled Gloucester fish the world over. This view is looking across to the Battery Wharf of Parmenter and Rice, fish dealers owned by the author's great, great Uncle George Garland. It is now part of the Building Center off Duncan Street.

ON HER MAIDEN SAIL, the handsome schooner *Selma*, launched by A.D. Story only two weeks earlier, glides out Gloucester Harbor for her trial run on Labor Day, 1904, under Captain Felix Hogan, with 200 guests. The sails were made by E.L. Rowe. Note mastheadman Wylie Rudolph working main topsail over to leeward of fore peak halyards. (Herman W. Spooner)

Three
Outward Bound

GOING FISHING on a summer southwesterly, a veteran clipper schooner rounds the new Eastern Point Breakwater about 1910 and heads into the Atlantic.

THE ITALIAN BARQUE *Nostra Signora del Boschetto*, with a cargo of salt for curing codfish, double-anchors in the Outer Harbor on an August day in 1912, while the crew takes to the yards to furl her vast squaresails. (Eben Parsons)

MORE SALT SAILS IN on August 8, 1912, in the 204-foot iron ship *Antares* of Genoa. The salt was probably taken on at Trapani, Sicily. Eben Parsons, whose family was in the salt business, gathered the dashing young crew up in the bow. (Parsons)

CARRYING TOO MUCH DRAFT to lie full-laden at Parsons salt wharf (behind her in East Gloucester), this unidentified salt ship anchors in 1898 in the "Deep Hole" of the Inner Harbor. Until light enough to dock, she's offloading into schooners that will sail salt to Maine fishing ports; her lower yards are cocked to clear their masts and rigging. (Blatchford)

THE THREE-MASTED SCHOONER *RALSTON* of Nova Scotia unloads from the Bahamian Turk Islands at Pew's salt wharf (now Gorton's) in 1920. Gloucester's salt-fishing schooners and processors consumed 32,000 tons from ten steamers in 1907 alone. (Gordon W. Thomas)

THE ONLY SIX-MASTED SCHOONER ever in Gloucester, the *Edward J. Lawrence*, a 320-foot, 2,483-ton ship built in 1908 in Bath, Maine, unloads in the stream in 1916. Eben squeezed in all but one mast. (Parsons)

A BUCKET HOISTED IN THE RIGGING by the cook summoned Captain Eli Cleaves, whose catboat *Aqua Pura* was a floating and advertising water tank. A hand pump and hose amidships handled the transfer to the departing schooner's water barrels. To a finicky landlubbing writer on a fishing trip in 1879, "the water [Eli] supplied was absolutely disgusting." (Blatchford)

DOING TRIPLE DUTY, it's hard to say if the steam towboat/lighter/water boat *Moses Adams* (built in Essex in 1885 by Moses Adams!) is nudging the old schooner *Noon Day* (built in Gloucester in 1873) into Parsons wharf or about to "water" her, while the trusty steam lighter *Philip* (below) spouts off doubling as the city's fireboat. (Martha Rogers Harvey and Spooner)

THE BIGGEST ICE HOUSE IN MASSACHUSETTS (236 by 210 feet with a capacity of 34,000 tons) was built by Francis Homans off Essex Avenue in West Gloucester in 1876. The city's fresh "market" fishery consumed over 40,000 tons of ice a year, in the schooners and ashore, not to mention kitchen iceboxes. Oysters made a cool sideline at 145 Main Street (below) in the days of their gustatory glory.

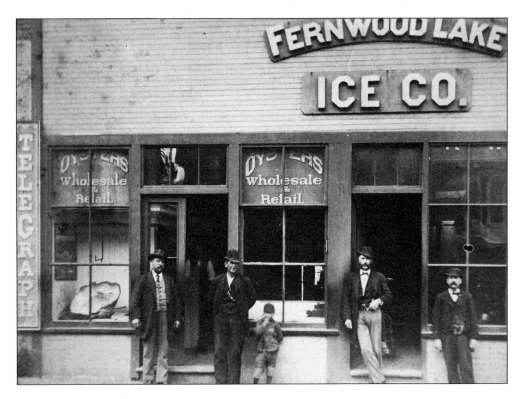

BAIT IS WHERE YOU FIND IT. Clammers wallow through the tidal mud flats of Jones Creek in West Gloucester, with the dunes of Coffin's Beach and Annisquam in the distance. As the insatiable demands of the hook-and-line fishery and retail market depleted the beds, Gloucester turned increasingly to herring. In the photograph below, 1,400 barrels of Newfoundland salt herring are being unloaded at the Slade Gorton wharf (today International Seafood on East Main Street) from the schooner *Columbia* in January 1927. In the background are Joe O'Brien (customs inspector), Matt Critchett (captain), and Ben Pine (an owner). (Harvey, JEG collection; CAHA)

THE MEMBERS OF THIS AMIABLE CREW, probably of Gloucester's deepwater Portuguese, haven't yet set about baiting their trawls, and may not until they get on the grounds, depending on the distance. A black derby hat was "right classy" a hundred years ago, but beware the soaring gull.

BAITING UP BEFORE SAILING implied a short trip to the nearby grounds, most likely for the fresh fish market in Gloucester or Boston. Herring, probably, has been chopped for bait on the top of the main cabin at right. (Blatchford)

"BAIT THE HOOK WELL: THIS FISH WILL BITE." So promised the Bard. And so baits the crew of the small schooner *Lafayette* at Chisholm's wharf (now Star Fisheries) in 1905. Each coil or "skate" of heavy tarred cotton trawl line ran about 1,700 feet, with 300 hooks on 3- or 4-foot, lighter "ganging" lines tied on every 5 or 6 feet. (Blatchford)

AN OLD HAND COULD BAIT AND COIL eight or nine hooks a minute. Halibut trawls and "ganjins" were the longest and heaviest, followed by cod and then haddock. Six to eight tubs of trawl to a two-man dory could stretch across two miles of ocean bottom. (Blatchford)

SAWIN' 'N' SPLITTIN', a husky young fisherman—perhaps not seasoned (or callous) enough to be the cook—pauses for the redoutable Martha Harvey a hundred years ago. When done, down the hatch to the galley stove. (Harvey)

TIME OUT FOR A PIPE. Cook Fred Lawson relaxes in the stern of Captain Jeff Thomas's 1906 schooner *Cynthia* about 1910 while one of the gang baits up.

WORKHORSES OF THE HARBOR, Gloucester in 1900 kept half a dozen steam tugs busy, among them the handsome 60-foot *Startle*, with a crew of four, built in town in 1889. Captain Nicholas Gangloff built the first of record in 1869, the diminutive *B.B. Gangloff*. (Blatchford)

WITH SPANKING NEW SAILS limp and still unstretched, the schooner *Russell*, just launched in Essex in 1913, is pushed busily past Rocky Neck by *Nellie* in search of wind for her maiden trip. (Blatchford)

ON HER OWN NOW, an unidentified old clipper is cast off in the Outer Harbor by the old tug *Joe Call*, built in Essex in 1882 by A.D. Story and named for one of the old-time sparmakers. No topmasts and a light crew imply they may be bound for Newfie after a trip of bait herring. (Spooner)

APPROACHING TEN POUND ISLAND past Eastern Point, Steam helpfully hauls Sail toward the oblivion of the future. (Spooner)

GHOSTING AND NIGH ADRIFT, the sails of Gloucester are silhouetted windless against the outer profile of Eastern Point and the tiny lighthouse keeper's cottage on Ten Pound Island (where Winslow Homer boarded and painted memorable water colors in the summer of 1880). (Harvey, JEG collection)

ON PAST THE PANCAKE GROUND the departing schooner sails to the sea. Here a fleet of coasting schooners, having made harbor for the night sometime around 1900, has anchored on the holding ground that parallels the Point shore, and dries canvas before getting under way again. (Chester N. Walen)

STANDING UP LIKE A STEEPLE, as the fishermen used to say, the knockabout *Natalie Hammond*, launched in December 1913, feathers along in her own reflection one shimmering day the following July. (Parsons)

FULL AND BY OFF THE POINT, the *Ida S. Brooks* tests the Atlantic. (Blatchford)

RAIL DOWN, WITH SPRAY FLYING, *Imperator* smashes through the chop off Gloucester during the filming of the classic motion picture *Captains Courageous* in 1937. (Doane Nickerson, Jr.)

OUTWARD BOUND is the 90-foot *Irene & May*, built in Essex in 1901.

Four
Dorymates

EVERYTHING ABOUT THE KNOCKABOUT *CATHERINE* WAS BIG—the heft of her crew, her 120 feet on the waterline, her skipper Archie MacLeod, and her record as a highline dory-trawler, halibuting and haddocking from 1915 to 1933.

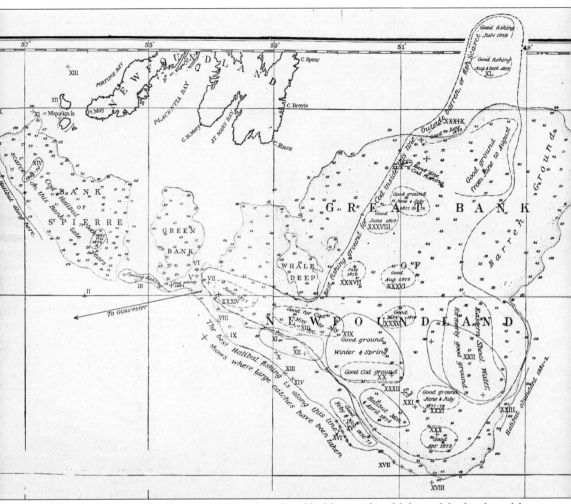

THE GRAND BANK WAS ALIVE with cod and halibut in the old days of the hook-and-line fishery under sail. (Goode)

WITH DORIES NESTED BOTTOMS-UP and lashed against boarding seas, foretopmast left behind, and the crew dressed for the cold, the giant *Tattler* is most likely bound for the banks. Beyond the end of her bowsprit a three-masted coasting schooner rides at anchor off Black Bess on outer Eastern Point. At right she charges along in the wake of the motorboat from which Ernest Blatchford snapped these 5x7-inch glass plate photographs. Built by A.D. Story in 1901 and said to have the thickest masts and biggest mainsail in the annals of the fleet, *Tattler* set the all-time dory-fishing record under Captain Alden Geele when she hailed into Gloucester one September day in 1916 with 500,000 pounds of salt cod worth $21,000. (Blatchford)

51

ON THE GROUNDS baiting up begins in earnest, during any weather, frequently day and night. Under Captain John Silveira with the bucket, the crew of the *Leonora Silveira* of the Gloucester Portuguese fleet, a "semi-knockabout" with short bowsprit, works through trawls and gangings in 1918. Wrecked twice and rebuilt as the *Pilgrim* and then *Shirley C.*, she starred in the movie *The World in His Arms* in 1951, a few months before she wrecked for the last time.

NOT SNOW, NOR RAIN, NOR HEAT, NOR NIGHT kept the doryman from his appointed course. This photograph was taken aboard the Gorton-Pew schooner *Corinthian* in 1936. (Edwin H. Cooper)

JOGGING UNDER FORESAIL IN A BRISK SEA, a Gloucesterman awaits fishing weather. The photographs on pages 53 to 57 were taken aboard *Onato*, a similar schooner, in about 1905 with a box camera by crew member Chester Morrissey, who was around sixteen at the time. (Chester L. Morrissey, JEG collection)

A MODEL FOR "THE MAN AT THE WHEEL," *Onato*'s helmsman holds her steady as you go. Later in life a skipper and seagoing balladier, Captain Morrissey loaned the author the negatives of these vintage photographs, remarking that his simple camera never let him down, even after he dropped it overboard once. He died in Gloucester in 1978 at the age of 90. (Morrissey)

A DECKLOAD of codfish has already been forked up as the dorymen return to *Onato* from hauling their trawls. (Morrissey)

"DOGGING AROUND," the gang thinks of home as *Onato* sails smooth seas back to Gloucester. (Morrissey)

NEARLY FIFTY YEARS AFTER ONATO, the schooner *Adventure* closes out the era of dory-trawling. In this *c.* 1950 photograph, the skipper is Leo Hynes, the photographer John Clayton. The first tub of trawl follows oars, spritsail, anchors, and flagged buoy. The aging dorymen will clamber in, to be dropped into the rushing sea by their mates at the dory tackles to the bow and stern beckets from the main and foremast heads. (John Clayton, The Gloucester Adventure)

FROM ONE NEST, THEN THE OTHER, *Adventure* drops her dories while under power in a "flying set," in contrast to the "standing set" when the schooner under sail alone hove to for the dorymen to row out in a radiating pattern to set their trawls. Hinged up against the jibstay is the bow pulpit to be lowered for the harpooner should a swordfish be spotted. (Clayton)

UNDERRUNNING THEIR TRAWL set skate-to-skate from the tubs for a mile or more—anchored and buoyed at both ends—the bow man hauls a fish over the spool-like roller on the gunwale while his mate carefully coils the line and hooks back in the tub. Hooks on a heavy trawl could catch and drag a man overboard, and even capsize the dory. (Clayton)

ALONE IN THE FOG, dorymates ply their trawl in the timeless fashion of fisherman and fish. (Clayton)

SPRITSAIL FLYING, one of her dories runs home to the Old Lady, as her affectionate crew called *Adventure*, while another is about to tie up alongside with a load of codfish. (Clayton)

SHARE AND SHARE ALIKE was the creed of the dorymates for a hundred years. Half of the profit of a trip went to the owners, while half went for equal division among the crew. It cut both ways: if a "broker," the boys came home with nothing. (Clayton)

IN WHAT WAS PROBABLY A RECORD one day in January 1943, *Adventure*'s twenty-four dorymen set and set again on Georges Bank for twenty hours straight, and hauled up, rowed in to the schooner, pitched up, dressed, and iced down 128,000 pounds of codfish, every one by hand. (Clayton)

JUST PLAIN TUCKERED OUT, dorymates up in the foc'sle of the schooner *Corinthian* dig into some chow and "flake out" with their boots on. (Cooper)

Five

The Georgesmen

THE SHOALS OF GEORGES BANK, at once Gloucester's treasure and source of eternal sorrow, are fearsome in a gale. This is the earliest known rendition of a schooner hove to on the great fishing ground, published by Procter Brothers in 1871.

WINTER WAS THE RICHEST FISHING, but it was often brutally cold: here, fifty Georgesmen, the most rugged schooners in the fleet, are frozen in solid in 1875. Breaking through the harbor, the steam tug *Vim* tows the schooner *D.E. Woodbury* through with a load of bait, probably frozen herring from Newfoundland.

HALIBUT FROM A RETURNED DORY TRAWLER are discharged at Union Fish on Parkhurst's wharf at the foot of Duncan Street. Five schooners and forty-eight men were lost in the first two months of 1875. By year's end the toll was sixteen schooners and one hundred and forty-three Gloucester fishermen.

WITH THE WINDLASS BROKEN BY THE SURGE ON GEORGES, the crew of the *T.L. Mayo* had to cut the cable to get home in February 1875. They must have decided to remove and repair the cabin top too, while frozen in. Carrying no dories, the handlining Georgesmen slung a small yawlboat from stern davits, which are shown here empty.

LOOKING OUT THE HARBOR, past the *Mayo* and the steam tug *Camilla*, the searching lenses of the stereoscope camera capture the end of Rocky Neck before the erection of its landmark Tarr & Wonson copper paint manufactory.

A TYPICAL "GEORGIE", the squat-sterned *Otis P. Lord* (built in Gloucester in 1876), crosses the harbor in the 1890s. The crew stand on the "reefing planks" between the stern davits during a blow while shortening the lower leech of the mainsail. Vertical reinforcing strips prevent chafing on the shrouds when the sails are out before the wind. (Blatchford)

AT THE RAIL ON GEORGES, Mr. Belly gaffs aboard a codfish while Mr. Burly jigs his handline against his "sojer" on the rail. Mr. In-between cuts out the tongue each saves and cashes in for his share; there was no share-and-share-alike on the Georges in the 1880s. (Goode)

MESSY DRESSING, the gurry goes overboard for the gulls, the livers into the basket for rendering into nutritious codliver oil back in Gloucester, and the fillet is split for icing or salting in the fresh or salt fish market. (Goode)

SAFE HOME FROM GEORGES BANK, *Canopus* scuds in past the Ten Pound Island light, past the now familiar Rocky Neck paint manufactury, and past the wee steam harbor ferry *Little Giant*. The men in their dories are probably "stream buyers" rowing out to bid for livers for oil and sounds for the city's isinglas factories. (Blatchford)

Six
Seines, Sloops, and Swordfish

(Martha Rogers Harvey)

Then it's laugh, "Ha! ha!" and shout, "Hurrah!" We are bound for the coast of Maine;
Our hold is well stored with salt and food, In the boat we've a fine new seine.

From "The Merry, Merry Mackerel Catchers"
The Fishermen's Own Book (1882)

NOT SO MERRY MACKEREL CATCHERS confront the camera with their poor old seine aboard an unidentified schooner. The ship in the background is probably a salt steamer.

TYPICAL OF THE GLOUCESTER SCHOONERS is the cabin of the mackereler *John D. Long* about 1880. Bunks clear around to the companionway at left, a potbellied stove and coal hod, clock and barometer high on the forward trunk, oilskins, sou'wester hats, and socks hung up to dry, and compass and oil lamp to the left of the companionway visible through the "binnacle peep" to the helmsman on deck and handy to the skipper's bunk, crew in attitudes of fatigue and boredom. (Goode)

BEFORE THE PURSE SEINE came into general use after the Civil War vast numbers of mackerel were caught by hook and line as the sociable New England fleet of "jiggers" followed the schools up the coast to the Bay of St. Lawrence from spring to fall. Here a crew "jig" with lines from which are suspended several baited, lead-weighted hooks called jigs, while one on the right "tolls" the prey toward the surface with a mush of ground-up bait. (Goode)

FROM THE MASTHEAD OF A SEINER a school has been spotted. Leaping into the seineboat, the crew strains at the oars to encircle it with the purse net before the wily mackerel dive and escape in a silvery flutter. (Goode)

71

LEAVING THEIR DORY to mark the start of the set, the mackerelers have surrouunded the school (they hope), racked their oars, and are putting their backs into pursing up the bottom of the net. (Goode)

REMAINING ABOARD, THE CAPTAIN AND THE COOK have sailed *Smuggler* (built in Essex in 1877) up to the pursed-in seine. Joined by a few crew, they pull the slacking net over the rail and bail mackerel on deck with the dip net hauled up via the tackle by the pair at the foremast. (Goode)

A FEW MERRY MACKERELERS FROM GLOUCESTER ride at anchor off Children's Beach, Nantucket, in 1920. (Charles F. Sayle collection)

BACK IN GLOUCESTER the seine is taken off a seineboat, probably for repairs, by the same old-timers that can be seen behind the young woodchopper on page 40. (Probably Harvey)

HOME WITH A DECKLOAD, the crew of the *Frank Foster* dress and salt their fare in a clutter of hastily furled sails, lines, gear, barrels, fish, and onlookers. The Gloucester mackerel pack in 1881 was 163,851 barrels. (Goode)

EVERYTHING FLYING, the 38-foot fishing sloop *On Time* sweeps home by Eastern Point from dory fishing about 1900. Some three dozen "sloop boats" fished the inshore grounds and occasionally beyond. Those with clipper bows and fine lines may have inspired the handsome "Friendship" models built at Friendship, Maine. (Blatchford). At right, overcoats, wool hats, derbies, heavy oilskins, mittens, and reefed mainsail say wintry weather for the sloop *Helen Pooler* dory-trawling. The high oval cockpit coaming gives the helmsman some protection. With only one mast, how did they get their small dories overboard and back? Pure heft, most likely.

LOOKOUTS ALOFT WITH A STRIKER AND HIS HARPOON at the ready in his bowsprit pulpit, an auxiliary schooner rigged out for swordfishing prowls along on a glassy sea, watching for targets near the surface. The doryman in the cap with the swordfisherman's long sun visor has rowed out and picked up the keg buoy attached to the harpoon line of a fish just ironed and is playing his dangerous prey. When the big fellow is

tired enough to bring to the surface, the gutsy fisherman will gingerly secure
him alongside with a line around his tail, and with the foghorn tucked there
under the thole pins signal the schooner to come alongside, finish him off,
and heist him up over the rail. Enraged swordfish occasionally speared the
bottom, capsizing the dory and sometimes wounding their tormenters.
(Albert D. Simmons, JEG collection)

KEEP CLEAR! If this not so docile-looking giant of four or five hundred pounds, just brought up from the dory alongside, had any life left he could clear the deck with that sword. The schooner is probably the *Leonora Silveira*. Market swordfishing in the days of plenty could provide an exciting summer's living for the lucky fishermen in small schooners and even sloops from New England fishing ports.

Seven

Back Home

GLOSTA COMIN' UP, a Georgesman sails in from the bank past the welcoming twin lights of Thacher's Island off Cape Ann's eastern shore. (Blatchford)

THE KING OF THE FLOUNDERS had yet to be dethroned by overfishing when this halibuter docked at the New England Fish Company on Dodd's wharf, across the slip to the east from the Boston and Gloucester Steamship wharf (now ORES). Manager Ernest Blatchford kept an eye

out and his camera handy. Halibut dorymen were known for their strength and endurance: they fished the heaviest gear on the longest trips in the biggest schooners under the hardest conditions for top prestige, if not dollar. (Blatchford)

"DRESSING HALIBUT ON DECK OF SCHOONER FOR ICING IN THE HOLD" claims the caption under this line cut of a vessel at sea in Goode's "Fisheries"—except that the photograph from which it was rendered, taken by T.W. Smyllie in 1882, shows them alongside a wharf (which has been eliminated). Perhaps Mr. Smyllie had no taste for the banks. (Goode)

SPLIT SALT CODFISH IS FORKED UP from the schooner, which has just arrived at what is probably Pew's (now Gorton's). (Spooner)

"HEY, WHAT'S YER STOCK?" All eyes and ears are turned to the nearest of the returning dory trawlers. The shoresmen are weighing out and washing a fare of salt codfish before resalting. New-looking "spiles" (never "piles" in Gloucester) and heavy planking indicate the wharf, probably on Rocky Neck across from Duncan's Point, is being extended. (Blatchford)

AS WATERTIGHT INSIDE AS OUT, a couple of dories double as tubs for washing cod being weighed off at Walen's wharf, now Star Fisheries. Rock ballast is piled behind the men, with an anchor cable beside the wheelbarrow. (Blatchford)

A MOUNTAIN OF SORRY-LOOKING FISH is forked through this unidentified wharf operation for salting and curing on the wooden outdoor racks called flakes. The codfish catch alone in 1887 was 58,190,900 pounds. Gloucester had the dubious "distinkshun" of being the leading manufacturer of fish glue from cooked skins.

FISH, HORSES, AND THE WIND ruled Boston's famous T Wharf at the turn of the century, shown in this view looking toward Atlantic Avenue. Gloucester schooners dominated the fleet that the towboats nursed in and out of one of the nation's biggest fish markets, occasionally hauling them between the ports in light airs. Competition to be first in for high price was fierce.

SPLITTING AND WASHING A TRIP OF CODFISH from the schooner *Evelyn M. Thompson* on Perkins wharf (now Gorton's) below Rowe Square on April 19, 1912. (Parsons)

FROM BANNER HILL ABOVE EAST MAIN STREET in 1912, Eben Parsons snapped two sweeping views down across the Reed and Gamage wharves (now Beacon Marine Basin) at the height of salt fishing, when real estate ran out and every roof flat enough was covered with fish flakes. The cloths protect the fish from "burning" in the heat of the day. A salt ship (above) and barque (below) lie at anchor in the Deep Hole. (Parsons)

THE EARLIEST KNOWN PHOTOGRAPH OF THE GLOUCESTER WATERFRONT was taken from the Belmont House hotel at 157 Main (then Front) Street in 1876 by William Elwell. Looking over flake-covered Clark wharf (later the world-famous Frank E. Davis mail order fish plant, now the vacant Gloucester Landing lot on Rogers Street), the photograph also shows Harbor Cove, the Fort, Ten Pound Island, the Outer Harbor, and the end of Eastern Point. (James B. Benham collection)

FLAKE YARDS SPRANG UP on every vacant waterfront lot, including this one off East Main Street. Behind the horse and wagon is the Methodist Church with its truncated steeple, which is still standing. Brown's Yacht yard is located down at the right. And how about that horseless carriage?

FIVE POUND ISLAND IN 1912 beyond East Gloucester's "Barbary Shore," is a place of abandoned fish houses, wharves, and vessels, fated in 1938 to be the terminus for the fill extending out from Smoky Point for the State Fish Pier at the end of Parker Street. (Parsons)

THE ELECTRIC TROLLEY RATTLES ALONG EAST MAIN STREET past the John F. Wonson fish wharf at exactly 10 a.m. on June 4, 1911, according to Eben Parsons's watch. The trolley's too-brief span on Cape Ann expired after only twenty-five years in 1920. Across Smith Cove are the twin tracks of the Rocky Neck Marine Railway. (Parsons)

DENNIS AND AYER ON THEIR WHARF AT THE FOOT OF PEARCE STREET (now the southwest corner of the Americold freezer on Rogers Street), was typical of Gloucester's fifty-four fishing firms in 1880, several of which owned fleets of schooners.

IMAGINE PUTTING IN A 10-HOUR DAY in 1909 or any other year, pulling bones from an endless school of leathery codfish with a pair of pliers—at how much an hour?

MR. SHUTE, OR PERHAPS MR. MERCHANT, stands sternly derbied and waistcoated in the well-ordered cutting and packing plant of Shute & Merchant, located on Parker Street (the current site of Montagnino's building and wharf). Their specialty was Georges codfish.

THE BIGGEST WHARF IN GLOUCESTER one hundred years ago covered an entire acre, and was owned by the Atlantic Halibut Company. The city's biggest fresh fish firm consumed 10,000 tons of ice afloat and ashore, and shipped up to five million pounds of the giant flatfish before halibut were virtually fished out, perhaps forever.

POSSIBLY THE UGLIEST STEAMSHIP EVER BUILT, the 142-foot *City of Gloucester* carried fish, freight, folks, and what have you every day of the year, weather be damned, from 1883 to 1925. Here she plows through the ice past the Rocky Neck Copper Paint Factory about 1910. (Blatchford). At the left, she is shown about to return on a summery day to Gloucester from her berth in Boston at 281 Atlantic Avenue. The captain will probably swing close aboard for his passengers to have a close look at the six-masted schooner which can be dimly seen beyond the towboat.

Eight

Taking In the Slack

SAILS SAGGING IN THE GLASSY CALM, schooners rest at Jordan's wharf (now Rose's east wharf) a hundred years ago. Mildew was cotton's worst enemy. The missing foreboom of the vessel at center is being repaired or replaced. The low-freeboard sloop *Wanderer* at right is a water boat. (Harvey)

VIEWED FROM ROCKY NECK in a time exposure in the 1870s, a portion of Gloucester's growing fishing fleet rides at anchor in the Inner Harbor awaiting, perhaps, nothing more nor less than a breeze.

FORTY-FIVE YEARS LATER, in 1919, the scene seems little changed, except that now the fleet is idled by a fishermen's strike. A mainsail droops in the tide from one of the Gorton's fleet, possibly not by accident.

DESTINY-BOUND, the great schooner airing her sails at the Fred L. Davis (now Seven Seas) wharf was built on speculation by Leonard MacKenzie, Jr., at the east end of Pavilion Beach and launched on August 31, 1901. One week later President McKinley was assassinated. His vice president succeeded him, and Davis bought the new vessel and named it *Theodore Roosevelt*. (Blatchford)

DARK AND WEATHER-BEATEN, the small schooner *Mizpah* (built by A.D. Story in 1894) lies at Walen's wharf drying her mainsail, and, over the rail, what may be some clothing. Across the wharf, topsails are brailed—more or less. The sail loft behind the end of the main gaff is probably Ben Cook's on Leighton's wharf.

ON A HARBOR AS STILL AS A MILLPOND, two old-timers from Essex commune and reflect: *Polar Wave* (built by Aaron Burnham in 1875), and the *Carrie E. Sayward* (built in 1870 by John James and Leonard MacKenzie the elder). Note the hollowed-log pump in the seineboat. *Polar Wave* was lost in 1901, but her crew was saved. (Harvey)

TUCKED UP IN HARBOR COVE just inside Fort Point, the *Porter S. Roberts* waits to sail, with a few of the crew taking in the slack in the stern. Beyond her mainmast is Gloucester City Hall, the old Baptist Church to its right. Rigged for Georges, the *Roberts* was built by Arthur Story in 1882 and abandoned at sea in a gale in 1894 by her crew, who were picked up in the dories. (Harvey)

JUST DRIFTIN' ALONG, a trim sloop boat not much bigger than her docile dory ghosts over the harbor. Her crew of two would as soon sail as fish, as who wouldn't on such a day so many years ago? (Spooner)

OH, WHAT A DAY FOR IT! Big sloops, small sloops, tiny sloops, catboats, cutters, dories, coasting schooners, a fishing schooner or two, and a big salt barque promenade the Outer Harbor one fine afternoon, probably in the 1880s. The western tip of Ten Pound Island can be seen, with Shag Rock on the left and Eastern Point beyond.

WHERE THE WIND LISTETH, there for the moment shall *Ingomar* follow, off the Magnolia shore outside the Harbor. Designed by Tom McManus and built by James and Tarr in 1904 as a big "Indianheader" (his spoon bow type, several of which were named for Indians), the *Ingomar* memorialized the hero of the play *Ingomar the Barbarian*, and lived up to it as a great fish killer. She lost four men over the years and was wrecked ignominiously on Plum Island in 1936. (Spooner)

SLOWLY THE FORESAIL LOWERS as the gang slacks off the halyards. The breakthrough *Fredonia* was conceived by Edward Burgess, the only rival of immortal yacht designer Nat Herreshoff, and built in Essex in 1889 by Moses Adams. Faster and more seaworthy than the old clippers, the elegant "Fredonia model" set a new trend for fishing schooners exemplified today in the replica *Spirit of Massachusetts*. Ironically, due to a construction failure, she sank in a storm in 1896 with two fatalities. (Harvey)

SWISHING ALONG ON A SUMMER AFTERNOON, the gleaming white excursion steamer *Cape Ann* churns from the Steamship Wharf at the foot of Duncan Street past Atlantic Halibut's glassed-in lookout for incoming vessels. The time was 3:30 p.m. on July 17, 1910, and a sunburned deckful heads back for Boston after a day of play on Fishtown's beaches. (Parsons)

LOBSTERS LIE LURKING among the half-tide rocks and seaweed off the western harbor shore. The way to see where you're going is on your feet, facing the bow, and pushing (not pulling) the oars, lobsterman fashion. (Spooner)

DORYMAN'S LUCK may lie in setting your trawl, not on the distant banks of Newfie, but in the middle of your own Harbor Cove, with the blessings of City Hall over your bow, of the Congregational, Unitarian, and Catholic Churches on the left, and of the Baptist on the right. (Spooner)

LITTLE FISHERS INTO BIG FISHERS GROW. At the head of Harbor Cove, the 1891 schooner *Emma & Helen* is shown at Mansfield's wharf, with the classic steeple of the first Universalist Church in America between her masts. (Harvey)

DOCK RATS AT LOW TIDE IN HARBOR COVE. Float and sundry boats are temptingly aground a hundred years ago. Kids are kids. (Martin Horgan collection, CAHA)

WHARF RATS ON A PRECARIOUS PERCH, with a former wharf rat perched precariously on the main gaff jaws of the schooner *Dorothy*. The author's namesake grandfather toppled into the harbor playing on a wharf in 1864, couldn't swim, was rescued by a passerby who heard his cries, praise be. (Blatchford)

TAKING THE OLD "SHORT CUT" HOME, Gloucester schoolboys in knickers or pants (depending upon age and therefore status) watch halibut being hoisted out at the New England Fish Company, the very same boys caught by Manager Blatchford on page 80. (Blatchford)

Nine

Winter

SAFE HOME through heavy seas and freezing spray with 17,000 pounds of halibut, the *Georgie Campbell* ties up at the New England Fish Company on February 27, 1900. Big ones could top 600 pounds. (Blatchford)

CRUNCHING THROUGH THE HARBOR ICE toward open water ahead, off winter fishing in February 1918, *Mariner* hauls the *John R. Bradley* past Ten Pound Island. The U.S. Fish Hatchery is visible just astern of the towboat.

A FRESH HALIBUTER RIDES IT OUT, anchored on the Grand Bank about 1880. No artistic license here. Captain Joseph W. Collins of the U.S. Fish and Fisheries Commission collaborated with H.W. Elliott, drawing from his experience as one of Gloucester's saltiest halibut skippers. (Goode)

"HALIBUT SCHOONER TRIPPED BY HEAVY SEA" is Captain Collins's caption. Under such conditions chances of surviving were pretty grim, and hundreds of Gloucester schooners didn't. His were among those that did. (Goode)

FROM THE LOOK OF THE ICE LINE on her starboard side, the *Clara G. Silva* rode into Gloucester on a southeaster. The dory about to be lowered suggests she'll anchor in the stream while the skipper rows ashore to talk price. (Walen)

DOWN ALMOST TO HER SCUPPERS with the weight of ice, a big trawler lies lumpily at Jordan's wharf in February 1919. In extreme cases, such topheavy schooners, laboring through a gale, simply capsized. (Parsons)

A WINTER WONDERSHIP? Captain Frank Rose of the *Natalie Hammond* (at left), with a couple of his crew, reflects on what might have been about 1937.

ONE OF THE OWNERS GOT HITCHED, and *Oriole* icily and windily celebrates in her own way. It's January 27, 1911, at Jordan's wharf, and the towboats have been keeping ahead of the ice. In 1916 *Oriole* would be rammed and sunk by a steamer in the fog, with four men lost. (Walen)

AH, THEM WERE THE DAYS. The old-fashioned winters in Gloucester were not without their compensations, in the middle of the Inner Harbor in January 1912, and around the same time in Smith Cove (below), looking toward Rocky Neck. (Parsons; Walen)

Ten

Shipshape and Gloucester Fashion

GRIPPING THE FORESTAYSAIL HALYARD WITH HIS LEG, a Gloucester rigger works around the base of the battens nailed to the foremast to take the chafe of the gaff jaws, c. 1900. The forestay loops around the heel of the foretopmast, over the spreader and around the foremasthead above him; the jibstay is above that, with the triatic stay to the mainmasthead off to the right. (Blatchford)

TWO PAGES FROM THE *1875 GLOUCESTER DIRECTORY* reflect the complexity of the fishermen's support system.

IN A RESPITE FROM HARD FISHING, the 1902 *Bertha and Pearl* is shown here hauled out of Smith Cove on the north track of the Rocky Neck Marine Railway for fix-up and a paint job. If he'd hauled her up before, the yard boss had the right bilge blocks on the cradle, and at high tide she would nudge comfortably into her old place and be pulled up the track by the steam engine. Beyond is the East Gloucester shore.

THE MARINE RAILWAY OF BROTHERS ELIAS AND PARKER BURNHAM had been at its present Harbor Loop location "over town" for at least forty years when the *Mabel Leighton* (built in 1884) and *Hattie B. West* (1860) were hauled out about 1889. Getting photographed at your work place was an occasion.

TIRED OLD *EDITH S. WALEN* GETS REHABBED on Burnham's. The stocky "Georgie" (built in Essex in 1884) carried 22 feet of beam on only 80 feet of waterline. Note the heavy cable required for anchoring in the rip tides of Georges Bank in the bow. The remaining brick ground floor of Burnham's grist mill today houses an ancient sawmill and electric hauling motor. (Blatchford)

ONE GOOD PUFF and the *Grace Otis's* sails will be in tatters. In this 1912 photograph even the patches have patches, and the main topsail and fisherman's staysail draped between the masts have holes. And how about crawling out on that swordfishing pulpit on the end of the bowsprit? Good luck. (Parsons)

PREPARING AN EYE SPLICE in heavy manila is no easy job without a fid to part the strands during a 1923 fishing trip aboard the very fast but ill-fated *Columbia*. Designed by Edward Burgess's son, the equally brilliant Starling Burgess, she was built that year as a contender in the Fishermen's Races with Canada. Note the unusually steep rise of her bow.

ARE THE MEN ABOUT TO SEND THE MAIN TOPMAST ALOFT, or have they just unshipped it there on the Cunningham & Thompson wharf at Fort Point? Note the one jiggling the halyards on deck. It's 1913. The *Louisa R. Sylva* was built in Essex in 1904 for Provincetown owners and has just been sold up to Gloucester. (Parsons)

THERE'S MORE THAN ONE WAY TO. . . To save the expense of hauling the old *Harvard* (built in 1891) on the railway, crew members about 1920 caulk a seam in the counter from a launch and paint her topsides from a raft at Jordan's wharf.

THE MYSTERY DEEPENS AS THE TIDE FALLS under the handsome but dishevelled *Sylvania* off the Head of the Harbor wharf of Sylvanus Smith. Built for this farsighted leader of the Gloucester fisheries in 1910 by John Bishop, the *Sylvania* was scuttled off Nova Scotia on August 31, 1918, by a German prize crew aboard a captured Canadian steam trawler. Is she careened for a fast bottom repair? The photograph gives no clue. (Spooner)

Eleven

Masters and Men

FIRST AMONG EQUALS on every Gloucesterman is the skipper, Ben McGray (in the necktie of course) of the *Lottie* G. *Merchant,* shown with some of the gang around ninety years ago.

THE SAYWARD BROTHERS—George, Epes, Jr., and Horace—sit still for the photographer about 1870. They ran the family fishery that extended clear around the foot of Point Hill in East Gloucester (an area from today's Lighthouse Marina to the Ben Smith Playground on East Main Street), and gave their name to Sayward Street.

THE OLD SALTS OF THE MASTER MARINERS ASSOCIATION of Gloucester are being entertained at Red Roof, the Eastern Point summer home of economist and future Congressman A. Piatt Andrew (fourth from left in the front, with the bow tie), in 1910 or 1912. "Doc" Andrew's close friend, the flamboyant art patron Isabella Stewart Gardner ("Mrs. Jack") of Boston, is the bundled-up lady second from his left. (Robert W. Phelps)

A MAN TO BE RECKONED WITH was Captain James William Pattillo, shown here in his retirement, who sailed up to Gloucester from Nova Scotia as a tempestuous young giant in 1834 and provided the author with escapades enough before and after to fill a book—which he did. (JEG, *That Great Pattillo*)

CAPTAIN AND MRS. WILLIAM H. THOMAS aboard the schooner *Thomas S. Gorton*, recently launched from the Tarr and James yard in Essex in August 1905. A colorful "bluenose" skipper from Arichat, Nova Scotia, Billy was a brother of Captain Jeff.

121

KING OF THE MACKEREL KILLERS, Solomon Jacobs was born in Twillingate, Newfoundland, in 1847. He had scanty schooling as a youth, but the year after he arrived in Gloucester in 1872 he was given command of a schooner. Tall, strong, intensely competitive, and innovative, he rose rapidly to the top of the mackerel fisheries, made and lost fortunes, and sailed as far as Irish waters in one direction and the North Pacific the other, opening up new grounds. He died in 1922 at the age of seventy-four.

THE FIRST BIG STEAM-POWERED VESSEL IN GLOUCESTER was his daughter's namesake, the *Alice M. Jacobs*, built for Sol in 1902 and shown here on her trial off Rocky Neck. She was a great success mackereling until December of the following year, when she was wrecked on a reef off Newfoundland in a gale. The crew was saved. (Blatchford)

CAPTAIN JACOBS'S MOST SPECTACULAR VENTURE was the impressive *Helen Miller Gould*, the first engine-powered schooner, launched from John Bishop's yard into Vincent Cove on March 29, 1900 (above), magnificent under full sail on her trial run in Gloucester Harbor on April 11 (below). The *Gould* showed the way for the practical introduction of the otter trawl, viewed by the hook-and-line fishermen even then as the sourge of the future. But seventeen months later, like the *Alice Jacobs* before her, she met her end—by fire at North Sydney, Nova Scotia, on October 25, 1901. The crew was saved, and Sol started all over again. (Blatchford)

CAPTAIN FRANK STREAM AND HIS BRIDE, Josephine Peterson, pose for their wedding portrait around 1885. Born in Sweden in 1860, like many of his countrymen he climbed rapidly to command in Gloucester. The *Florence E. Stream* and *Waldo L. Stream* were named for his children. A highline halibuter, he died in 1935.

ONE OF A THOUSAND FISHING CREWS of Gloucester musters around its skipper, standing there in his companionway in his pinstriped Sunday pants, for the sake of an anonymous posterity.

WATCHING AND WAITING, with his dories out, Captain John Silveira keeps close to the wheel of the *Leonora Silveira*.

PORTUGUESE FISHERMEN FROM THE AZORES, among the hardiest and most daring in the North Atlantic, began emigrating to Gloucester before the Civil War. These men are in the Georges cod fishery about 1880. (Goode)

IDENTIFIED AS FISHERMEN'S HOMES IN GLOUCESTER around 1880, one wonders how many could afford even such modest houses. Retaining much charm, many remain around the city. (Goode)

THIS SALOON AND CIGAR EMPORIUM at 44 Main Street in the West End features a whole windowful of the clay pipes favored by working men of the 1890s. The number of bars in Gloucester fluctuated wildly from year to year as the city voted now wet, now dry. (Corliss & Ryan photograph)

A FEW DOORS UP, AT 96 MAIN STREET, is the popular Olympic Billiard Parlor. According to Fitz McIntosh, proprietor, the parlor was "fitted up in a neat style, and parties wishing to play a cozy game of Billiards are invited to call. The best of order is preserved, and everything first-class, including Bailey's New Patent Cushion Tables." (Corliss & Ryan)

"CENTENNIAL" JOHNSON THEY CALLED HIM, after his dory. "A damned fool," he called himself after surviving the first solitary crossing of the Atlantic in history, to celebrate the centennial of American independence. Alfred Johnson was a twenty-nine-year-old Dane and had been a Gloucester fisherman for ten years when on a dare he ordered a custom-built sailing dory from Higgins & Gifford and departed alone for Britain on June 15, 1876. In the face of incredible odds he made the Welsh coast after fifty-nine days at sea. (JEG collection)

LANDBOUND IN HIS RETIREMENT, Captain Johnson exhibited *Centennial* and himself on tour for Gorton's Fisheries, whose schooners he skippered during a successful career as a master. He died in 1927 at the age of eighty-two. His famous dory is on display in the Cape Ann Historical Museum. (JEG collection)

THE GREATEST GLOUCESTERMAN was Howard Blackburn, shown here at home in July 1883 after surviving five days in a dory in January without food or water when he and his dorymate, who froze to death, were separated from the *Grace L. Fears* (see page 14) during a blizzard on Burgeo Bank. The Nova Scotia native rowed 65 miles to the coast, losing all his fingers to frostbite, and returned to Gloucester a hero. He eventually became a legendary saloonkeeper, and in 1897 he organized an around-the-Horn goldmining expedition to the Klondike. He then tackled the Atlantic a third time, journeying solo in the 30-foot sloop *Great Western* to Gloucester, England, in sixty-two days. (JEG, *Lone Voyager*)

TUNING UP FOR PORTUGAL in June 1901, the "Fingerless Navigator," now forty-one, tests his 25-foot sloop *Great Republic* in the harbor. He reached Lisbon in thirty-nine days, a record crossing that stood for decades. A third attempt, at a round trip in a sailing dory, was aborted by storms that almost took his life. After other astonishing feats, the "Lone Voyager" died in bed at seventy-three in 1932. *Great Republic* lives on in the Cape Ann Historical Museum. (*Lone Voyager*)

NEITHER CAPTAIN NOR CREW, the cussed independents have always been the day fishermen of Cape Ann from Magnolia to East Gloucester, along the Annisquam River to Squam, round the Back of the Cape on Ipswich Bay to Rockport and Sandy Bay. This old geezer back in great-grandpa's time caused some amusement stepping from his dory into the mud of Lane's Cove.

Twelve

The Romance of It

"HOW DOES SHE RIDE? WHY, SHE SHAMES THE GULLS!" So said the skipper, gripping his wheel with fists of steel as he eyed the cut of his jib. The pride o' Gloucester in the 1930s, the *Gertrude L. Thebaud* spreads her racing wings offshore. (Adolph Kupsinel, JEG collection)

HEAVE! HEAVE! HEAVE! and up goes the mainsail as a picked crew from Gloucester under Captain Martin Welch prepares to sail the schooner *Esperanto* to Halifax to accept a challenge for a series of Fishermen's Races between Canada and the United States (meaning Gloucester) in November 1920. Under way (below), old hands prepare to send the fishermen's staysail aloft to give her a little more drive in the light air. (*Pathe News*, Louis Martin Welch collection, CAHA)

ALONG FOR THE RIDE AND A YARN is James Brendan Connolly, the South Boston winner of the first gold medal of the modern Olympics in Athens in 1896, whose novels and short stories picked up where *Captains Courageous* left off, making Gloucester fishermen and their schooners heroic and romantic figures. (Welch collection)

PICK-UP RACING BETWEEN SCHOONERS, where the first home won top price, was formalized with the tempestuous free-for-all known as "The Race That Blew" in 1892, sailed off in a full gale to celebrate Gloucester's 250th anniversary of incorporation. When an America's Cup match was called off because of rough seas in 1920, the disgusted publisher of the *Halifax Herald and Mail* flung the gauntlet for a REAL race between REAL sailors and REAL working vessels for $5,000 and a silver cup. Gorton-Pew Fisheries accepted, and their *Esperanto* beat Nova Scotia's *Delawana* two straight and returned with the silver—for the first and last time. Lunenburg, Novie's chief fishing town, built the giant *Bluenose* in 1921 to the limit of the agreed-upon dimensions, 112 feet on the waterline, and 143 feet stem to stern. Gloucester's *Elsie* (only 106 feet on the waterline and 124 feet stem to stern, and therefore inherently slower) under Marty Welch, won the eliminations but lost the cup. The Americans came close but never regained it from *Bluenose*, immortalized by the Canadians on their dime. The age of sail ended sadly, occasionally bitterly, yet gloriously with the nostalgic final series between *Bluenose* and the *Gertrude L. Thebaud* in 1938, on the eve of World War II.

THE ONLY GLOUCESTER WINNER OF THE CUP, Captain Marty Welch (and wouldn't you know it, a Novie!) shares his wheel with a crew member for the cameraman aboard *Esperanto* en route to Halifax. The following May *Esperanto* was wrecked on Sable Island, her crew saved—by none other than the *Elsie*. (Welch collection)

OOPS! In rough seas off Halifax during her first race with *Bluenose* on October 22, 1921, *Elsie* snaps her foretopmast. The whole rig goes by the board, and the six men sent out on the bowsprit to haul in the flogging balloon jib hang on for dear life, buried by a big one. (W.R. Macaskill photograph, JEG collection)

134

CONTROVERSY BLEW around the lanky figure of Captain Clayton Morrissey of the *Henry Ford*, designed in 1922 (as was *Puritan*) as much to beat *Bluenose* as to meet fishing requirements. But *Puritan* was lost on Sable Island. The *Ford* bested the *Elizabeth Howard* under Captain Ben Pine and the *L.A. Dunton* (now at Mystic Seaport, Connecticut); but—amidst a storm of recriminations—she barely lost to *Bluenose*, and in 1923 and 1926 lost the trials to *Puritan*'s successor, *Columbia*. In 1928, she was wrecked off Newfoundland, but her crew was saved. (Kupsinel, JEG collection)

SURGING ONWARD with a gala crowd, the *Arthur D. Story* presents a tableau of grace and power, but failed to win the 1929 trials off Cape Ann. No matter; the races were called off anyway. (Kupsinel, JEG collection)

PLAYING TO THE GALLERY, mastheadman Charlie Landry, with the lofty job of tending topsails, squirrels along the spring stay from foremast to main, 80 feet or so above the deck, probably of the *Henry Ford*.

AND A SPARROW HE IS. That's Jack Sparrow at the mainmasthead of the stately *Columbia*, at left, probably as the ill-fated schooner defeated the *Ford* and the *Howard* in the elimination race of October 21, 1923.

THE LAST OF THE GLOUCESTER SCHOONERS to slide into the Essex River was the *Gertrude L. Thebaud*, appropriately from the yard of Arthur D. Story in 1930 for a syndicate that dreamed of wresting the cup from the overpowering *Bluenose* and her wily skipper, Captain Angus Walters. Designed by Payne, Belknap and Skene and named for the wife of her principal backer (Gloucester summer resident Louis Thebaud), she was very close to the dimensions of

Gloucester's nemesis, without the big Novie's famous upthrusting bow. Many people thought that the bow, a last-minute change in Canadian designer William Roue's plan (in order to heighten her focsle), gave *Bluenose* an extra turn of speed. (Kupsinel, author's collection; George Salter photograph, Dana Story collection)

LEGGO THAT MAIN SHEET! The gang rushes aft to spill the wind from the mainsail and help Ben Pine hold her helm down as the 148-foot *Elizabeth Howard*, the famous White Ghost of the Maine Coast, barely veers away from the anchored destroyer to slip astern of a rival vying for the starting line. The uniquely white *Howard* started as an extra-long McManus knockabout in Boothbay Harbor, Maine, in 1916, and after freighting salt fish got a bowsprit when she changed to fishing under a New York hail. She was wrecked off Nova Scotia a month after the 1923 trial.

YIKES! The main boom of the *Thebaud* barely clears *Bluenose*'s shrouds during the 1938 match. The Canadian crewman smiles: if the wood but kisses, it's a foul, and the Yanks lose this one.

ANOTHER CLOSE ONE. Closehauled, the *Thebaud* smashes by. The tall crewman at the rail under the wheel is probably Sterling Hayden, a big kid who loved to sail and was destined for Hollywood fame, fortune, and misfortune. (JEG collection)

LEADING *BLUENOSE* FOR A CHANGE, the *Thebaud* won this match in October 1938 but lost the grand finale of the International Fishermen's Races. Forty-five years later Sterling Hayden, the tall blond navigator with the binoculars and the compass, wrote these identifications under the photograph for the author (from left to right): "Jack Watson, Plutocrat JG, State Street Trust; Stuart Cooney, Sailmaker; Marian Cooney, Sailmaker

Extra Ordinaire [Stuart's father]; Captain Cecil Moulton; Honest Tom Horgan, AP, JEG Mentor [Horgan reported the races for *The Associated Press* in Boston, secured the handsome Hayden the film test that vaulted him into the movies, and in 1947 broke in the author as an AP reporter]; Harry Eustis [in white cap] 'Haul, you bastards, Haul!'; Hayden." (JEG collection)

A PAIR OF MASTER PROMOTERS were the occasionally friendly captains Ben Pine of Gloucester, a former junk dealer, and Angus Walters of Lunenburg, a banks fisherman, here aboard *Columbia* the day after she barely lost to *Bluenose* on October 29, 1923. Newfie-born "Piney" had a keen sense of business and publicity and was occasional "racing skipper" aboard challengers he had a part in building and managing. Howard Chapelle thought the abrasive Walters "an aggressive, unsportsmanlike and abusive man, but a prime sailor."

IN A FROTH AND A FURY *Bluenose* drives to overtake the *Thebaud* and take her wind in the bargain in a tense moment during the 1938 races.

IN NO RACE, BUT A GALA, the *Thebaud* lazes along off Eastern Point with a crowd that obscures the helmsman. The mastheadman commands his perch on the main crosstrees. (Kupsinel, JEG collection)

FULL AND BY, the *Gertrude L Thebaud* brings a lump to the throat as she closes 315 years of fishing out of Gloucester under sail with a frothing

bone in her teeth and every stitch of canvas drawing. (Kupsinel, JEG collection)

COLUMBIA THE GEM OF THE OCEAN the fishermen called her with tears in their eyes. She was designed by Starling Burgess and built by Arthur Story in 1923 to replace the lost *Puritan*. Even faster than her sister? The fastest, swore Jim Connolly: "The most beautiful schooner I ever saw. Coming bow on in a smooth sea and a fresh breeze--to see her so, viewing her from under her lee bow, and the way she had of easing that bow in and out of the sea—well, the beautiful lady was Poetry herself then." (Kupsinel, JEG collection)

Thirteen
Requiem

MEMORIAL DAY, 1921. Seven months after winning the first International Fishermen's race *Esperanto* struck a submerged wreck while fishing near Sable Island Bar off Nova Scotia. Her crew of twenty-one took to the dories and were rescued by the *Elsie*. Twenty-five years later the *Bluenose* was wrecked on the coast of Haiti; in 1948 the *Gertrude L. Thebaud* went down off the Venezuelan coast.

MEMORIAL DAY, 1928. The schooner *Mary* has just blown up at the wharf of Ben Pine's Atlantic Supply Company (now Fishermen's Wharf) below Hancock Street. The lighter *Philip* is lifting cabin and deck wreckage to retrieve the body of Captain John Farrell, the only casualty. That winter the *Mary* was rebuilt as the *Arthur D. Story* (see page 135). An era in twilight: note the amputated bowsprits of the schooners converted to dragging.

NOVA SCOTIA'S FOGGY, SHOAL-GIRT SABLE ISLAND was known as the "Graveyard of the Atlantic." Here lies the hulk of the *Lizzie M. Stanwood* in 1904, her salvaged mainboom hitched to a double yoke of oxen.

150

BACK HOME TO DIE. *Claudia* was the pride of the Sylvanus Smith fleet when she was launched from John Bishop's yard on Vincent Cove in 1902. (Walen). After a career in the fisheries she was sold to New Bedford for whaling in 1917, then to the Cape Verdeans as a packet, returning home after hard service in 1926. Laid up, a fisherman bought her for $7, and she rotted behind the old North Shore Theatre, a few yards from her birthplace, until 1939, when her remains were broken up. She now lies interred under the Rogers Street parking lot.

THEY THAT GO
DOWN TO THE SEA
IN SHIPS
1623 — 1923

Fourteen
Resurrection

NEWBORN, the 121-foot knockabout schooner *Adventure*, designed by Tom McManus and just launched for Captain Jeff Thomas from the James yard in Essex on September 16, 1926, lies in Gloucester awaiting her spars. (The Gloucester Adventure)

IN HIS SUNDAY BEST, ham-fisted Jeff Thomas poses on the wheelbox of his schooner *Cynthia* in 1910. (The Gloucester Adventure)

OFF DORY-TRAWLING, *Adventure* diesels out of Gloucester Harbor in 1937 under Captain Leo Hynes, who took her over when Jeff Thomas died at sea while chopping ice from the rigging in 1934. Minus her mainboom, there's room over the wheel for the shelter of a pilot house. Her topmast hardware remains a reminder of the days of full sail. (The Gloucester Adventure)

154

LEO THE LIONHEARTED. From 1934 to 1953, when he laid her up as the last American vessel still line-trawling (his men were aging, and the young guys disdained the hardship), Captain Hynes brought *Adventure* and her twenty-six dorymen through thick and thin, competing to the end with the overpowering draggers and their bottom-sweeping nets, which he disdained. In the war year of 1943 the "Old Lady" made forty-seven trips and stocked $364,000. In the photograph below, she shoves off from the Boston Fish Pier about 1950, the Customs House Tower the only highrise on the skyline. Captain and Mrs. Hynes (both hail from Fortune Bay, Newfoundland) were living in New Hampshire in 1995, where he was going on ninety-five. (John Clayton, The Gloucester Adventure)

A SENTIMENTAL JOURNEY it was for the late schooner historian Gordon Thomas, Captain Jeff's only son who had never sailed the schooner he named as a boy, shown here taking his father's wheel from her owner/skipper Jim Sharp one day in June of 1982 for a sail down Penobscot Bay. Three partners bought *Adventure* in 1954 and ran her as a "dude" schooner along the Maine coast until 1965, when Captain Sharp bought and restored her to sailing trim and gave thousands of passengers the thrill of their lives on weekly summer cruises out of Camden for the next twenty years. (Tom Hoyne photograph, The Gloucester Adventure)

UNDER HER LOWERS ALONE, with reefed mainsail, and dressed in a yachty white, *Adventure* knocks off about 13 knots along a rocky Maine shore on a breezy summer day in the early 1980s. (Mike Anderson, The Gloucester Adventure)

HOME AT LAST and back in her fisherman's black, *Adventure* was returned to Gloucester in 1988 by Captain Jim Sharp as his gift to The Gloucester Adventure, a nonprofit group organized to restore her for the education of the public and as a symbol of the city's fishing heritage. In 1994 the National Park Service designated the old schooner a National Historic Landmark. She was then sixty-eight years old. (Fred D. Bodin, The Gloucester Adventure)

ARETHUSA, OUT O' GLOUCESTER, 1921. (Robert W. Phelps)

Epilogue or Epitaph?

The armada of canvas is hull-down over time's horizon. Its successor fleets of diesel-driven draggers and seiners are being grounded, with many others the world around, by the consequences of the global fishkill and of the still unfathomed depth and breadth of land-based pollution beyond the ability and will of largely indifferent national governments and world order to come to grips with. The toll continues: in September of 1994 the large steel Gloucester dragger *Italian Gold*, defying foul weather in search of an ever diminishing catch, was thrown violently to the bottom near Georges Bank with her crew of four fishermen.

Sometimes grimly, sometimes with wry humor, something about the spirit of Gloucester hangs on, something of its people, of its ghostly sails, and of the ways of fishing that transcend time and technology. Gloucester will remain uniquely Gloucester just as long as it remembers where it all came from, remembers its horrible, beautiful past, its people, its boats with their spirits of the wind, and the ways of the past that form the ever-more fragile mosaic of what it persists in being.

We who have been lucky enough to discover Gloucester deep somewhere in ourselves had better pray that it will hang on and on around us, if only as a sunset dying in the night . . . yet not that even, unless we keep on calling up and sharing mind's-eye memories of what we have no memory of—or do we?— as a people and a race, which may be all one can ask or expect of archeologists and self-appointed historians.

JEG

Sources

No photographic retrospect of Gloucester can be achieved without reliance on the collections of the Cape Ann Historical Association, the core of which was assembled over a lifetime's study of our sailing heritage by my friend and mentor Gordon W. Thomas, son of Captain Jeff, and acquisitioned shortly before his death. Others over the years from whom I've absorbed fathoms of history and lore include the late Captain Bill Sibley, Charlie Sayle, Al Flygare, Jim Brennan, Charlie McPhee, and Marty Horgan; Captains Tom Morse, George Byard, Joe Santapaola, Leo Hynes, and Frank Mitchell; and Dana Story, Phil Bolger, Lorraine Louannis, and Jeff Thomas II. Nor would there be a book at all without the generous cooperation of president Harold Bell, administrator Judith McCullough, librarian Ellen Nelson of our "Historical," who granted me rare fishing rights and assisted with the angling, the excellent editing of Michael Guillory, and the bright idea in the first place of Kirsty Sutton.

For Further Reading

Chapelle, Howard I. *The American Fishing Schooners: 1825–1935*. New York, 1973.

Church, Albert C., and James B. Connolly. *American Fishermen*. New York, 1940.

Dunne, W.M.P. *Thomas F. McManus and the American Fishing Schooners: An Irish-American Success Story*. Mystic, CT, 1994.

Garland, Joseph E. *Adventure: Queen of the Windjammers*. Camden, ME, 1985.

————— *Down to the Sea: The Fishing Schooners of Gloucester*. Boston, 1983.

————— *Eastern Point*. Peterborough, NH, 1971.

————— *The Gloucester Guide*. Rockport, MA, (1973) 1990.

————— *Guns Off Gloucester*. Gloucester, MA, 1975.

————— *Lone Voyager*. Rockport, MA, (1963) 1995.

————— *That Great Pattillo*. Boston, 1966.

Goode, G. Browne et al. *The Fisheries and Fishery Industries of the United States*. Washington, 1887.

Kipling, Rudyard. *Captains Courageous*. New York, 1896.

Pierce, Wesley G. *Goin' Fishin'*. Salem, MA, 1934.

Procter Brothers. *The Fisheries of Gloucester*. Gloucester, MA, 1876.

————— *The Fishermen's Own Book*. Gloucester, MA, 1882.

Story, Dana A. *A Catalog of the Vessels, Boats and Other Craft Built in the Town of Essex 1870 through 1980*. Essex, MA 1984.

Thomas, Gordon W. *Fast and Able: Life Stories of Great Gloucester Fishing Vessels*. Gloucester, MA, 1973.

————— *Wharf and Fleet*. Gloucester, MA, 1977.